THE LITTLE BOOK OF

WINE

TIPS

Andrew Langley

THE LITTLE BOOK OF

WINE

TIPS

Andrew Langley

A.

'Fan the sinking flame of hilarity
with the wing of friendship; and pass
the rosey wine…'

Dick Swiveller
'The Old Curiosity Shop'
by Charles Dickens

1. Make your own wine vinegar by pouring any wine leftovers into the dregs of an old vinegar bottle. This will contain enough 'starter' (or 'vinegar mother', as it's called) to convert it into vinegar.

"Make your own wine vinegar by pouring any wine leftovers into the dregs of an old vinegar bottle."

2. To enjoy them at their best, **serve sparkling wines very cold.** The bubbles stay smaller and last longer at low temperatures (about 5°C or 40°F).

"Serve sparkling wines very cold."

3.

Bottle of red wine not finished?
To keep it in good condition use a vacuum pump to remove the air inside. This cheap and simple device stops oxygen from altering the wine's flavour.

"Bottle of red wine not finished?"

4. **Drink champagne** and other sparkling wines **from tall, thin glasses.** This gives the 'fizz' less chance of escaping than a wide, short vessel, and allows you to enjoy the sight of the bubbles rising to the top.

"Drink champagne from tall, thin glasses."

5. Make sure all wine glasses are completely clean. This precaution is not just to help you appreciate taste and colour at their best. **Residues of washing-up liquid, as well as fats, acids and even lipstick, can cause a sparkling wine to go flat very swiftly.**

"Residues of washing-up liquid, as well as fats, acids and even lipstick, can cause a sparkling wine to go flat very swiftly."

6. **Store your wine somewhere cool and very slightly humid.** Too much heat will speed up the chemical changes in the bottles, and probably cause off flavours. The best temperature is between 10 and 15°C (50–60°F). A slight moisture keeps the corks from drying out and shrinking.

"Store your wine somewhere cool and very slightly humid."

7. **Bottles should be stored on their sides.** This ensures that the wine covers the cork, keeping it wet. This prevents the cork from shrinking, and discourages the development of mouldy 'corked' aromas.

Bottles should be stored on their sides.

8. **Keep white and sparkling wines in the dark.** Bright light will spoil their condition and give them a sulphurous smell when opened. It doesn't do reds much good either.

Keep white and sparkling wines in the dark.

9. **You may find tiny bundles of crystals at the bottom of a bottle of wine. Don't worry.** These are only caused by too much tartaric or oxalic acid in the wine. They are completely harmless, and show that the wine has a good level of acidity.

"You may find tiny bundles of crystals at the bottom of a bottle of wine. Don't worry."

10.

Matching wine to food can be a fascinating exercise. Basic guidelines suggest red wines with meat and cheese, white with fish and dessert. Yet **there is plenty of room for amazing – and unexpected – combinations.** Try a sweet white such as Sauternes with Roquefort cheese or a Beaujolais with charcuterie and other preserved meats.

"Matching food to wine can be a fascinating experience. There is plenty of room for amazing – and unexpected – combinations."

11.

Choose wine glasses which are as plain as possible. Part of the delight of wine-drinking is appreciating in its colour, and this is lost if you put it in blue or pink glasses. Engraved or cut glass can also distort the subtleties of a wine's appearance.

Choose wine glasses which are as plain as possible.

12.

Drink your wine from glasses with wide bowls and narrow openings. The wine's bouquet will be concentrated at the opening, allowing you to stick your nose in and savour it to the full. If it's too wide (the opening, that is), some of the precious aroma will be lost.

Drink your wine from glasses with wide bowls and narrow openings.

13. When poured, the **wine should fill about one third of the glass** or less. This leaves plenty of room to swill the liquid about gently so that it will mix with oxygen in the air and develop its flavours more fully.

"Wine should fill about one third of the glass."

14.

Ensure that your wine store is just warm enough. **Excessive heat will spoil a wine, but excessive cold can do even more damage.** Anything under -4°C (25°F) may freeze the wine and even crack the glass bottle.

"Excessive heat will spoil a wine, but excessive cold can do even more damage.

15.

Most red wines are best served at room temperature. However, this is not a hard and fast rule. Average room temperature today is much higher than it used to be, so the wine will benefit from being a few degrees under. Some light reds, such as a Beaujolais, can even be served slightly chilled.

"Most red wines are best served at room temperature. However, this is not a hard and fast rule."

16. **When using wine in cooking, remember to boil off the alcohol content first.** The alcohol in warmed-up wine can taste harsh, but it will quickly evaporate when simmered over a moderate heat.

"When using wine in cooking, remember to boil off the alcohol content first.

17.

Several sauce recipes include a large quantity of red wine. However, **a wine rich in tannins can taste too acidic when reduced and concentrated by cooking.** Overcome this by including some chopped meat or meat stock in the sauce. The proteins in these will take away the harshness.

A wine rich in tannins can taste too acidic when reduced and concentrated by cooking.

18.

Don't worry if pieces of cork fall into the wine when you are opening a bottle. This has nothing at all to do with the wine being 'corked'. The bits can easily be fished out and have no effect on the taste.

"Don't worry if pieces of cork fall into the wine when you are opening a bottle.

19. If you have not finished a whole bottle, keep the leftovers in the refrigerator. **Once a bottle of wine has been opened, it begins to react with the air.** The coldness of a fridge will slow down any reaction, even with a red wine.

"Once a bottle of wine has been opened, it begins to react with the air."

20.

Allow a red wine time to breathe after opening. Simply removing the cork will achieve little, because of the tiny area exposed to the air. It's much better to pour the whole bottle into a glass jug, so that air mixes with all of it (very fine reds need a more delicate touch though).

"Allow a red wine time to breathe after opening."

21.

To decant a fine wine or port with a sediment, first leave the bottle standing up for 24 hours so that the sediment sinks to the bottom. Then make sure that the decanter is clean and dry. Tip the uncorked bottle gently as you pour: do not shake it, and do not stop pouring until the sediment has nearly been reached. A candle or lamp underneath helps here.

"To decant a fine wine or port with a sediment..."

22.

Opening a bottle of sparkling wine can be messy – and even dangerous if the cork flies out unexpectedly. **Hold the bottle at a 45° angle, directing it away from other people.** Take off the wire muzzle. Then grab the cork and hold it still while you gently turn the bottle with the other hand. This allows the cork to come out slowly. Have a glass at hand to catch any froth.

"Opening a bottle of sparkling wine can be messy... Hold the bottle at a 45° angle, directing it away from other people."

23.

Push the cork in if you are having major difficulties getting it out of the bottle. This is a last resort, but may be the only solution if the cork is broken or jammed. Then decant the wine into another vessel, holding the cork out of the way with a long thin implement such as a skewer.

Push the cork in if you are having major difficulties getting it out of the bottle.

24.

Before getting to work with the corkscrew, **always remove the foil from the bottle top.** This is usually either plastic or soft metal, and can be easily cut round just below the lip of the bottle. Then give the top a wipe to get rid of any residue.

"Always remove the foil from the bottle top.

25.

The best way to chill a bottle of white wine is to place it in a container filled with ice and water. This method takes only about 30 minutes, as opposed to about two hours in a refrigerator.

"The best way to chill a bottle of white wine is to place it in a container filled with ice and water.

26.

Sometimes you may need to warm up a bottle of red wine to room temperature. Don't do anything violent, such as plonking it on a radiator or stove top. **If you're in a hurry, warm a glass jug with hot water,** dry it thoroughly and decant the wine thither. Warmed glasses work even better.

"Sometimes you may need to warm up a bottle of red wine... If you're in a hurry, warm a glass jug with hot water."

27.

Serve a sweet, full-bodied white wine with most desserts. **The sweeter the dish, the sweeter the wine should be** (in general). Dry whites usually taste thin and acidic when drunk with sweet foods.

"The sweeter the dish, the sweeter the wine should be.

28. **The order in which wines are served can make a difference to how they taste.** There are three basic rules. Drink dry wines before sweet ones, young wines before old ones, and less good wines before fine ones.

"The order in which wines are served can make a difference to how they taste.

29.

The waiter's friend is one of the most reliable and simple of corkscrew types. Fold out the corkscrew and lever from the penknife-like handle. Screw the 'worm' into the cork, then engage the lever on the bottle lip and press upwards. The cork should come out smoothly.

"The waiter's friend is one of the most reliable and simple of corkscrew types.

30.

The first part of tasting a wine is done with the eye. Rotate the glass and study the wine to judge its colour and clarity (a haziness often denotes a spoiled flavour). **'Tears' forming on the side of the glass show that there is a high alcohol content.**

'Tears' forming on the side of the glass show that there is a high alcohol content.

31. **To appreciate the 'bouquet' of a wine, follow these steps.** Rotate the wine in the glass to mix in air. Then take a thorough (but gentle) sniff at the top of the glass, where the aroma will have gathered. Take time and concentrate on the different elements you smell.

"To appreciate the 'bouquet' of a wine follow these steps..."

32.

Get as thorough a taste of the wine as you can at the first mouthful. **Make sure you swill the liquid right round your mouth, so that it reaches all the different sensory areas.** Don't forget – once you've swallowed, it's gone. There are no taste receptors in the throat.

"Make sure you swill the liquid right round your mouth, so that it reaches all the different sensory areas."

33.

Wine is an essential ingredient in many marinades. It is very good at tenderising some meats and giving them extra flavour. A typical marinade for beef might also contain carrots, onions, garlic, seasoning and olive oil. Beware of marinating for longer than a few hours, or the meat will dry out, due to the acid in the wine.

Wine is an essential ingredient in many marinades.

34.

Poach fish or chicken in a white wine court bouillon. Simmer half a bottle of wine with a litre (2 pints) of water, chopped onion, carrot and celery, three bay leaves and a little wine vinegar. After 30 minutes, allow to cool. Drain the liquid and poach your fish in it. Even after this, the court bouillon can be used to make a fish soup.

Poach fish or chicken in a white wine court bouillon.

35. **The easiest gravy of all can be made by deglazing the roasting pan with wine once the meat has been removed.** The wine dissolves all those dried-up remnants of the juices and other meaty bits, and will eventually thicken a little as it reduces. Add salt and pepper to taste.

"The easiest gravy of all can be made by deglazing the roasting pan with wine once the meat has been removed."

36.

Lost the cork? **You can seal an unfinished bottle of wine with plastic wrap,** held in place with a rubber band. But don't leave it for longer than a day or two.

"You can seal an unfinished bottle of wine with plastic wrap."

37.

When cooking with wine, use stainless steel or enamel pans.
The acid in the wine will react with materials such as aluminium or untreated cast iron to produce an unpleasant taste. With aluminium this can also be dangerous to health.

When cooking with wine, use stainless steel or enamel pans.

38.

The better the cooking wine, the more tasty the dish. Don't be tempted to cook with only the crummiest and cheapest wines available. Their poor quality will be detectable in the end result.

"The better the cooking wine,
the more tasty the dish.

39.

To get rid of red wine stains on the carpet, sponge the spot with soda water or sparkling mineral water and blot it dry with a cloth. Then treat the area with a good carpet shampoo (but don't scrub). Rinse it out thoroughly and leave to dry naturally – perhaps with the window open.

"To get rid of red wine stains on the carpet...

40.

Wine stains on clothing or table cloths can be very hard to remove. One successful treatment uses a mixture of liquid dishwasher soap and hydrogen peroxide. Apply this to the stained fabric and leave to soak for an hour. Then put it through a gentle cycle on the washing machine.

"Wine stains on clothing or table cloths can be very hard to remove."

41.

A wine basket is used to hold the bottle at an angle while opening it for decanting purposes. It is certainly not something to use for pouring the wine out of.

"A wine basket is used to hold the bottle at an angle while opening it. "

42. **Keep your wine glasses stored the right way up.** Shelving them upside down may keep out dust, but it can also give them a stale 'cupboardy' smell which could affect the wine.

Keep your wine glasses stored the right way up.

43. Mulled wine is a cheering drink on a cold winter's day. Use a decent wine for it: **rubbish wine is still rubbish even when mulled.** Put 110g (4oz) of white sugar and a bottle of red into a large pan (enamel or stainless steel). Then add lemon zest, a cinnamon stick, 3 cloves and a pinch of mace. Heat very slowly to retain as much alcohol as possible. Serve in warmed glasses.

"Rubbish wine is still rubbish even when mulled."

44. **Spiced wine served cold makes an unusual aperitif.** In a glass demijohn, mix 3 bottles (or about 2 litres) of white wine with 2 cinnamon sticks, a vanilla pod, half a nutmeg, the peel of 4 oranges and 450g (1lb) of sugar. Then add 300ml (½ pint) of vodka. Cork it and leave for a month. Then strain into bottles and leave for another month before drinking.

"Spiced wine served cold makes an unusual aperitif."

45.

Most people have enjoyed a glass of kir, made with white wine and cassis. **A more unusual but even more delicious version,** drunk in southern France, **combines red wine with raspberry liqueur.**

"Most people have enjoyed a glass of kir. A more unusual but even more delicious version combines red wine with raspberry liqueur."

46.

Tired of eating strawberries with cream and sugar? Try strawberries in wine instead. Put 450g (1lb) of hulled strawberries in a glass bowl and sprinkle over 3 tablespoons of sugar. Add the juice of a lemon, a dash of cassis and about one quarter of a bottle of good rose wine. Put in the refrigerator for an hour before serving.

"Tired of eating strawberries with cream and sugar? Try strawberries in wine instead."

47. **A champagne sorbet makes a splendidly extravagant dessert.** Boil up a syrup of 300ml (½ pint) water and 250g (9oz) sugar, add the zest of one lemon and leave to cool. Mix in half a bottle of champagne, plus the juice of one lemon and one orange. Freeze, stirring every two hours and beating in 2 egg whites. Drink the rest of the bottle while waiting.

A champagne sorbet makes a splendidly extravagant dessert.

48.

Keep bottles of white wine out of the fridge until a few hours before you drink them. Days or weeks at artificially low temperatures will only deaden the wine's taste and aroma.

"Keep bottles of white wine out of the fridge until a few hours before you drink them."

49.

Walnut leaves have an amazing aroma all their own, **which can be captured in walnut leaf wine.** Soak a good handful of fresh, young, walnut leaves in 300ml (½ pint) of eau-de-vie or vodka for two weeks, then strain. Dissolve 200g (7oz) of sugar in about 1 litre (2 pints) of light red wine, then mix with the strained liquid. Mature in corked bottles for two weeks before drinking.

"Walnut leaves have an amazing aroma which can be captured in walnut leaf wine.

50.

Hippocras is a very ancient form of spiced wine (named after Hippocrates, father of medicine). In a bowl, mix a bottle of white wine, a glass each of white port and sherry, 4 tablespoons of honey and two glasses of armagnac. Add a cinnamon stick, 3 cloves and some nutmeg and black pepper. Leave for 24 hours, then strain and bottle.

"Hippocras is a very ancient form of spiced wine."

Andrew Langley

Andrew Langley is **a knowledgeable food and drink writer.** Among his formative influences he lists a season picking grapes in Bordeaux, several years of raising sheep and chickens in Wiltshire and two decades drinking his grandmother's tea. He has written books on a number of Scottish and Irish whisky distilleries and is the editor of the highly regarded anthology of the writings of the legendary Victorian chef Alexis Soyer.

"**A knowledgeable food
and drink writer.**"

Little Books of Tips from
Absolute Press

Aga	Gardening
Allotment	Gin
Avocado	Golf
Beer	Herbs
Cake Decorating	Spice
Cheese	Tea
Coffee	Whisky
Fishing	Wine

If you enjoyed this book, try...

THE LITTLE BOOK OF

BEER

TIPS

> "Beer makes an excellent marinade for some meats (and even some fish)."

> "Beer can be heated or 'mulled' and flavoured with spices."

Absolute Press

An imprint of Bloomsbury Publishing Plc

50 Bedford Square	1385 Broadway
London	New York
WC1B 3DP	NY 10018
UK	USA

www.bloomsbury.com

ABSOLUTE PRESS and the A. logo are trademarks of Bloomsbury Publishing Plc

First published in 2005
This edition printed 2017

A catalogue record for this book is available from the British Library.
Library of Congress Cataloguing-in-Publication data has been applied for.
ISBN 13: 9781472954480

Printed and bound in Spain by Tallers Grafics Soler